Written by   Linda Milliken
Design by   Wendy Loreen
Illustrated by   Barb Lorseyedi
Cover illustration by   Mella Cathleen

© 1992 **Edupress** • PO Box 883 • Dana Point, CA 92629

ISBN 1-56472-009-8

2

TABLE OF CONTENTS

TEACHER'S GUIDE

OBJECTIVES
- Practice and master a cutting skill.
- Complete a related project.
- Display the results.

By following these three steps, students learn that practice *does* lead to success!

BEFORE YOU BEGIN
- Show students the correct way to hold a pair of scissors. Check all hand positions before any cutting takes place. Habits learned correctly will be carried throughout the school career and facilitate cutting success.

USING THE BOOK

Skills Checklist (page 4)
- Use as a tool for tracking small motor development.
- Use as a planning guide for aides or volunteers working with children who need specific skill and motor coordination practice.
- Refer to individual progress for report card preparation and parent conferencing.

Practice Pages (pages 5-11)
- Reproduce pages for skill practice prior to beginning a project.
- Conserve paper by printing on the back of unused school newsletters, worksheets and other paper extras that would otherwise be thrown away.
- Encourage children to color practice pages before cutting. Not only will they develop coloring skills and refine hand movement but the cut pieces can also be glued in random patterns to colorful construction paper for an eye-catching art project. Store all extra pieces in a box or bag for use in other projects requiring paper scraps and trims.

Project Pages (pages 12-71)
- *Pattern*—Reproduce for project completion. Any patterns requiring tracing are noted in the project steps.
- *Skill*—Lists cutting skills needed for successful project completion.
- *Steps*—Lists sequential steps for completing pictured project.
- *Suggestions*—Each project may be varied or changed to adapt to time constraints, ability level and available supplies. The suggestions add to the project's visual appeal. They also develop other small motor skills such as pasting, finger painting, handling a paintbrush, rolling and curling. Encourage creative freedom. Allow students the opportunity to make project suggestions.
- *Literature Link*—Precede or follow the pattern project with a read-aloud activity. All literature selections are age-appropriate. Substitute another title if suggested book is unavailable.

Display
- The projects lend themselves to bulletin board and other classroom displays. Walls, doors and windows all make excellent project showcases. Be sure to feature all student efforts.

SCISSOR SKILL CHECKLIST

STUDENT NAME	SKILL	Solid straight	Dotted straight	Fringing	Zigzag	Angles	Circles (large)	Circles (small)	Spirals (large)	Spirals (small)	Curves	Scallops

PRACTICE PAGES

Solid straight lines

─────────────────────────

─────────────────────────

─────────────────────────

─────────────────────────

─────────────────────────

Dotted straight lines

- - - - - - - - - - - - -

- - - - - - - - - - - - -

- - - - - - - - - - - - -

- - - - - - - - - - - - -

- - - - - - - - - - - - -

Large & small circles

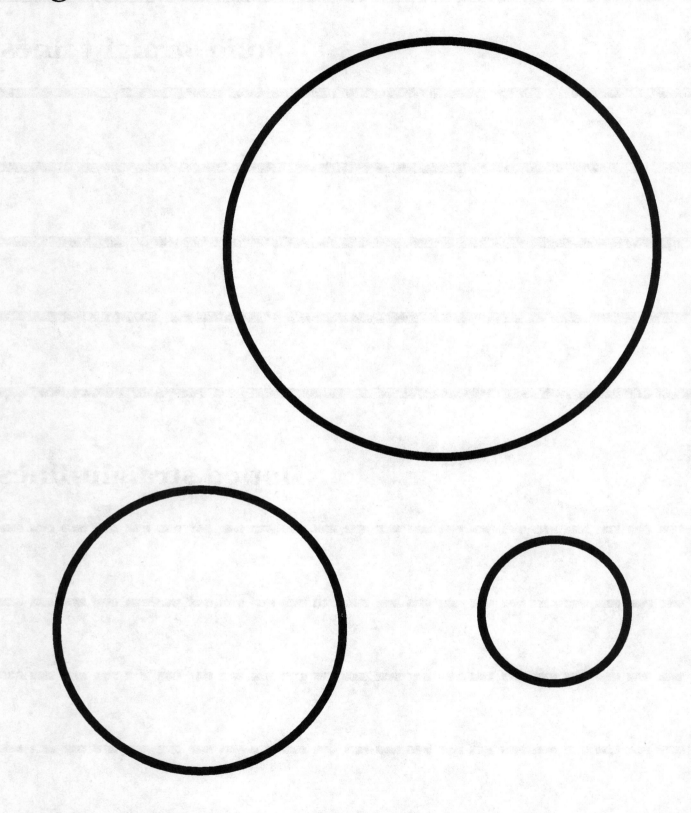

Scallops

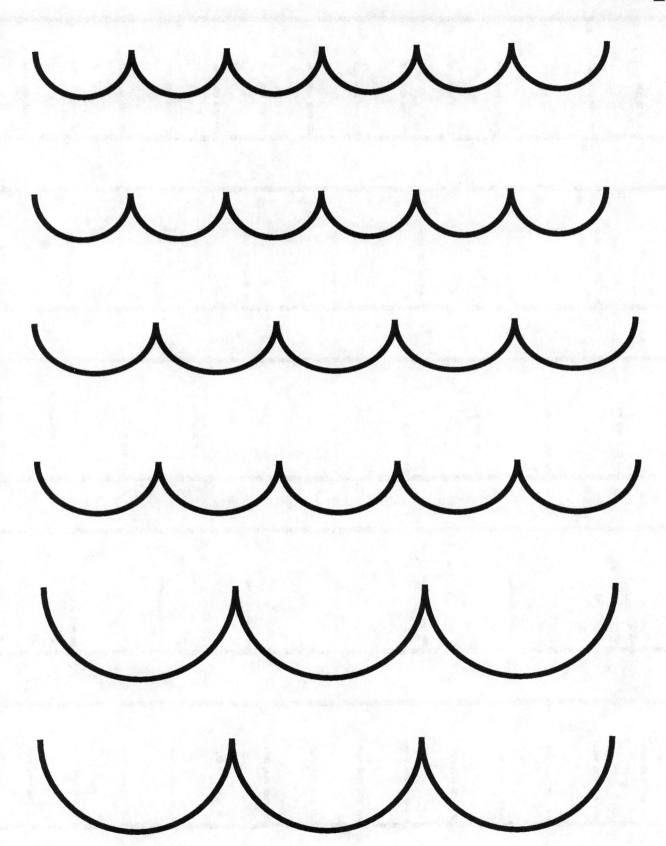

Fringing

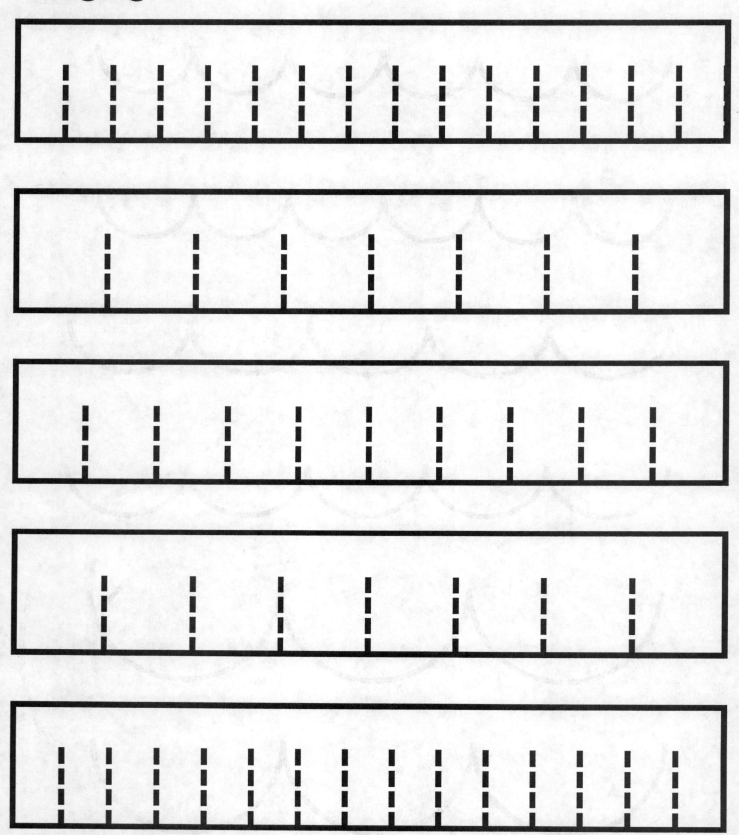

Large & small spirals

Curves

Zigzag lines

Angles

FALL

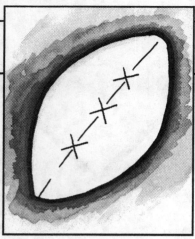

FOOTBALL

Skills: Large curves
Steps: Cutting, painting, gluing
Suggestions: Sponge paint brown. Glue white yarn or ribbon for stitching.
Literature Link: *Tackle*
                    by Louise M. Foley
    Herbie becomes a substitute player on a football team.

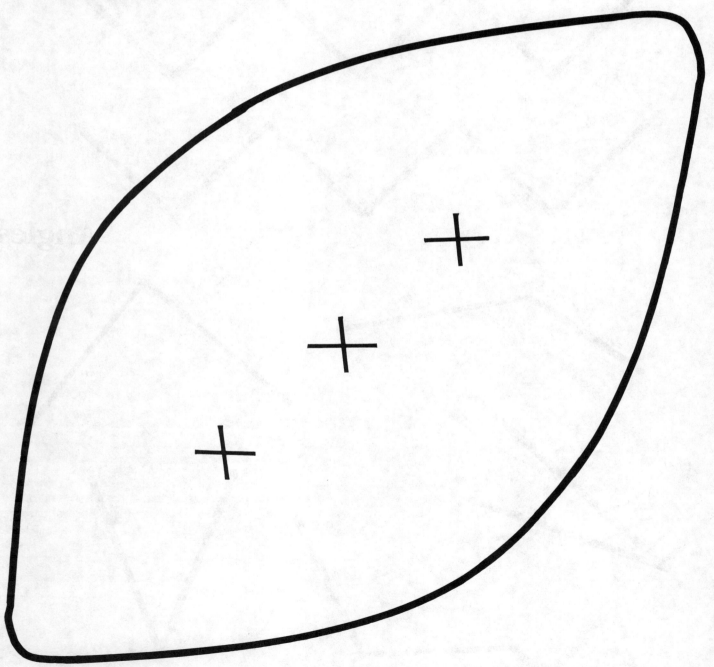

CRAYON

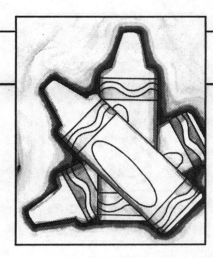

FALL

Skills: Straight solid lines, angles

Steps: Cutting, coloring

Suggestions: Make several crayons, each a different color. Use for recognition activities.

Literature Link: *Harold and the Purple Crayon* by Crockett Johnson.
Boy takes a walk on an imaginative walkway.

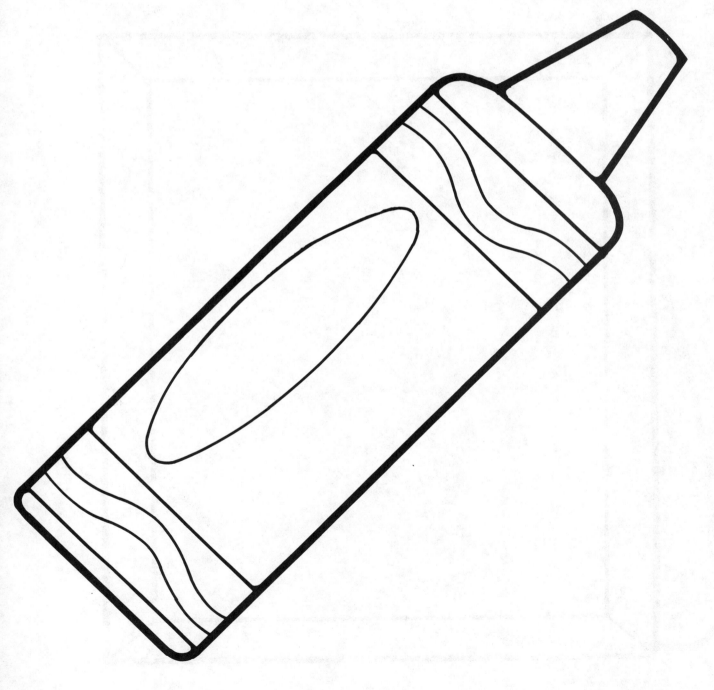

FALL

PICTURE FRAME

Skills: Solid straight lines
Steps: Cutting, coloring, pasting
Suggestions: Paste pictures of family or friends inside the frame.
Literature Link: *Pig Pig and the Magic Photo Album*
by David McPhail
 Pig Pig finds himself transported into a photographer's pictures.

LEAF

FALL

Skills: Large curves
Steps: Cutting, coloring
Suggestions: Use fall colors of orange, red, gold and brown to color leaf.
Literature Link: *When Dad Cuts Down the Chestnut Tree*
by Pam Ayres
The cutting of a tree means no leaves to rake—but no tree house either.

FALL

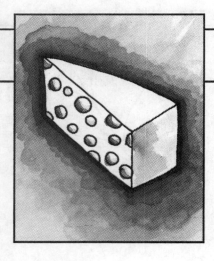

CHEESE

Skills: Solid straight lines
Steps: Cutting, coloring
Suggestions: Color yellow swiss cheese. Punch holes.
Literature Link: *The King, the Mice and the Cheese*
    by Nancy and Eric Gurney
  The king calls on wise men to stop the mice from eating his cheese.

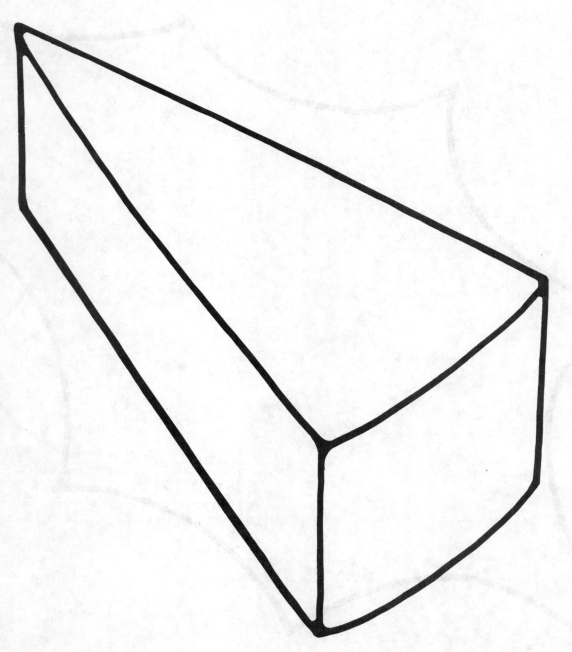

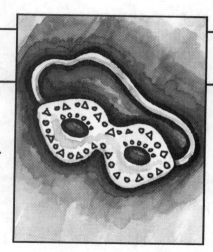

FALL

Skills: Large curves
Steps: Cutting, gluing
Suggestions: Decorate with trims. Cut eye holes.
Attach a band to fit the head.
Literature Link: *Shaggy Dog's Halloween*
by Donald Charles
Shaggy Dog has a problem with making a
Halloween mask.

FALL

JACK O'LANTERN

Skills: Large curves
Steps: Cutting, coloring
Suggestions: Color a face to turn the pumpkin into
a jack o' lantern.
Literature Link: *The Biggest Pumpkin Ever*
by Steven Kroll
Two mice hope to grow the largest pumpkin ever for
Halloween.

BLACK CAT

FALL

Skills: Circles, small angles
Steps: Cutting, painting, pasting
Suggestions: Paint a black cat. Paste parts together. Add a yarn tail.
Literature Link: *Rotten Ralph's Trick or Treat* by Jack Gantos
   Ralph the cat and a waitress exchange identities at a Halloween party.

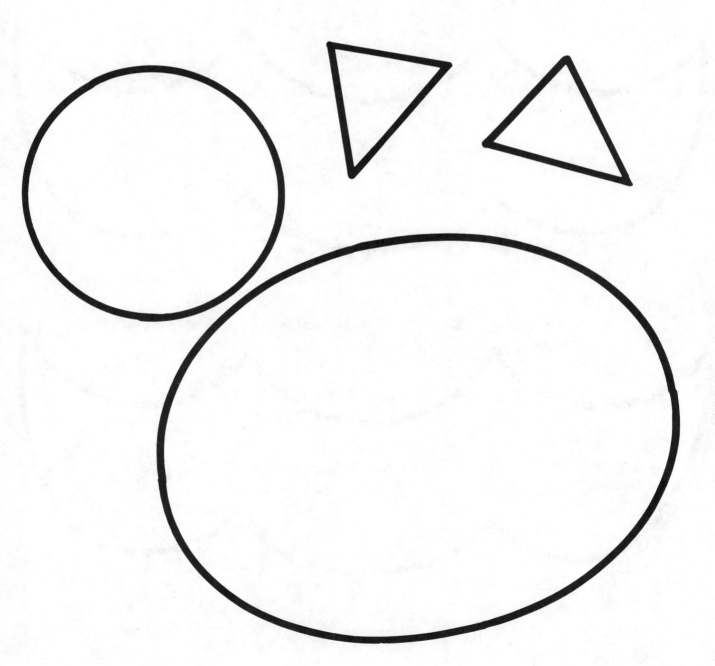

FALL

OCEAN WAVES

Skills: Scallops

Steps: Cutting, painting, gluing

Suggestions: Paint a ship to sail in the waves. Glue waves to construction paper.

Literature Link: *Jack, the Seal and the Sea* by Gerald Aschenbrenner

Jack rescues a seal who leads him to fishing grounds.

GHOST

FALL

Skills: Curved lines, large spiral
Steps: Cutting, coloring
Suggestions: Use puffy paints to make eyes "pop out".
Literature Link: *Birdy and the Ghosties* by Jill Paton Walsh.
A small girl meets a trio of ghosts.

FALL

ITCH

Skills: Angles, fringing
Steps: Cutting, gluing, coloring, curling
Suggestions: Color a face and a black hat. Glue together as shown. Curl fringed hair.
Literature Link: *S. Rickety Witch*
by Maggi Davis
A sweet old witch experiences a special Halloween.

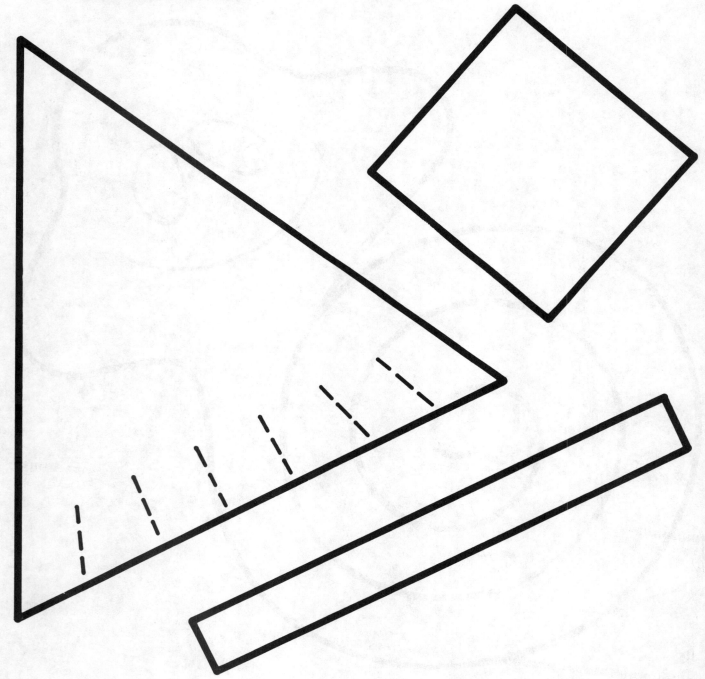

PILGRIM HAT

Skills: Solid, straight lines
Steps: Cutting, coloring, pasting
Suggestions: Color a yellow buckle; paste in place. Draw a face on a paper plate; paste under the hat.
Literature Link: *Pilgrim Children Come to Plymouth* by Ida DeLage

The Mayflower's children spend their first year in New England.

FALL

EAR OF CORN

Skills: Large curves
Steps: Cutting, coloring, gluing
Suggestions: Glue kernels of popcorn to the ear of corn.
Literature Link: *Corn is Maize; The Gift of the Indians*
by Aliki
Describes the origin of corn and how it is harvested.

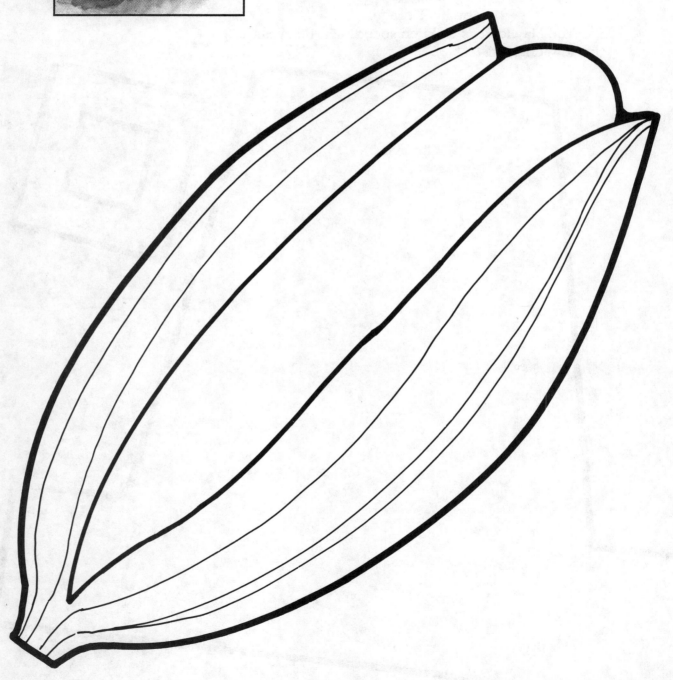

TURKEY

Skills: Scalloped circles, small circle, small curves
Steps: Cutting, coloring, pasting
Suggestions: Glue the turkey together. Staple a straw to create a handle for a puppet.
Literature Link: *One Tough Turkey; A Thanksgiving Story* by Steven Kroll
   The turkeys don't feel that the Pilgrim's should have had turkey on Thanksgiving.

FALL

FALL

CORNUCOPIA

Skills: Large curves
Steps: Cutting, coloring, gluing
Suggestions: Glue magazine pictures of fruits and vegetables to the opening.
Literature Link: *One Terrific Thanksgiving* by Marjorie W. Sharmut
  Irving Bear searches for holiday food and learns the true meaning of Thanksgiving.

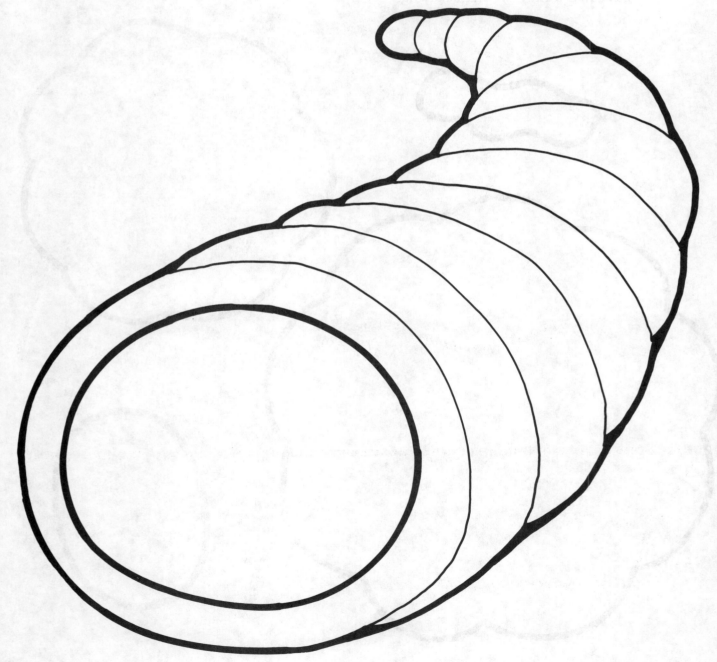

TASTY PIE

FALL

Skills: Solid, straight lines, large curve
Steps: Cutting, gluing, coloring
Suggestions: Show what kind of pie this is by gluing fruit, or other, cut-outs to the top crust.
Literature Link: *Chester Chipmunk's Thanksgiving* by Barbara Williams
  A chipmunk invites his friends to share his Thanksgiving pie.

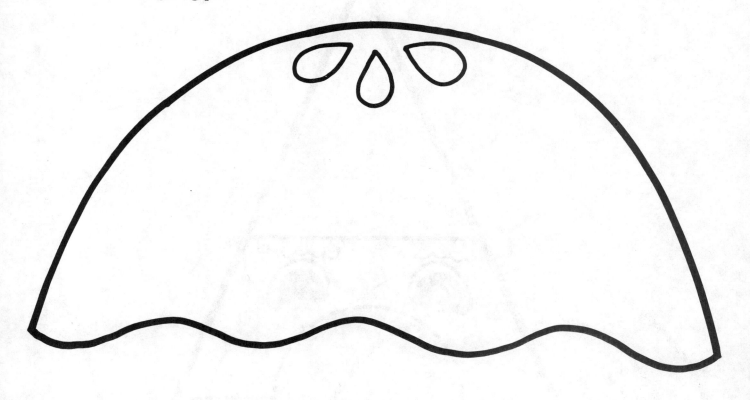

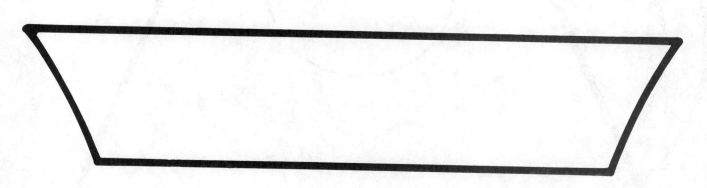

WINTER

SANTA

Skills: Straight lines, small circle
Steps: Cutting, coloring, pasting
Suggestions: Color a red hat; paste a cotton beard; cut on dotted line; hang on a doorknob.
Literature Link: *The Secrets of Santa*
by Annie Civardi
An exclusive interview with Santa himself.

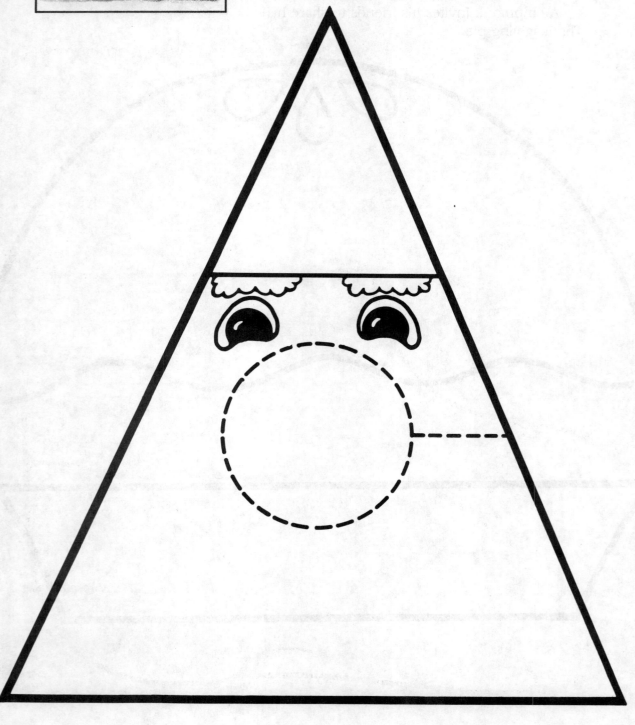

Stocking

WINTER

Skills: Large curves
Steps: Cutting, coloring, stapling
Suggestions: Cut two stockings. Staple the edges. "Stuff" with pictures
Literature Link: *Fat Santa*
by Margery Cuyler

On his way to fill stockings, Santa gets stuck in the chimney.

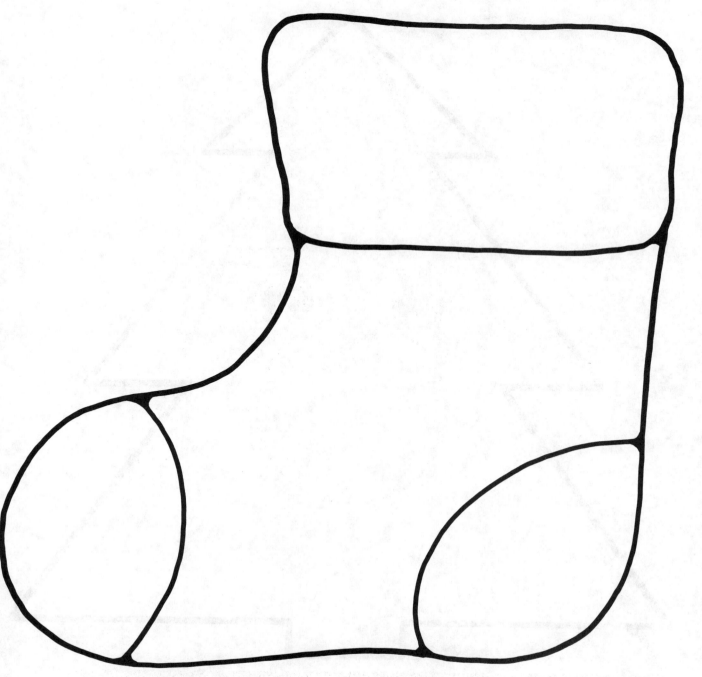

WINTER

HOLIDAY TREE

Skills: Angles
Steps: Cutting, painting, gluing
Suggestions: Paint a green tree. Sponge paint white flocking *(optional)*. Glue trims.
Literature Link: *A Christmas Story*
by Mary Chalmers
   A girl, a dog, a cat and a rabbit work together to trim the Christmas tree.

CANDLE

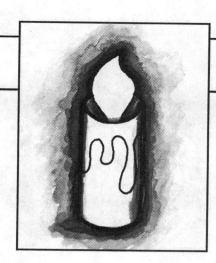

WINTER

Skills: Solid, straight lines, small curves
Steps: Cutting, coloring, rolling, pasting
Suggestions: Roll the candle to form a tube.
Paste to hold. Glue flame in place.
Literature Link: *A Candle for Christmas*
                by Jean Speare
A Canadian tale about a Christmas promise.

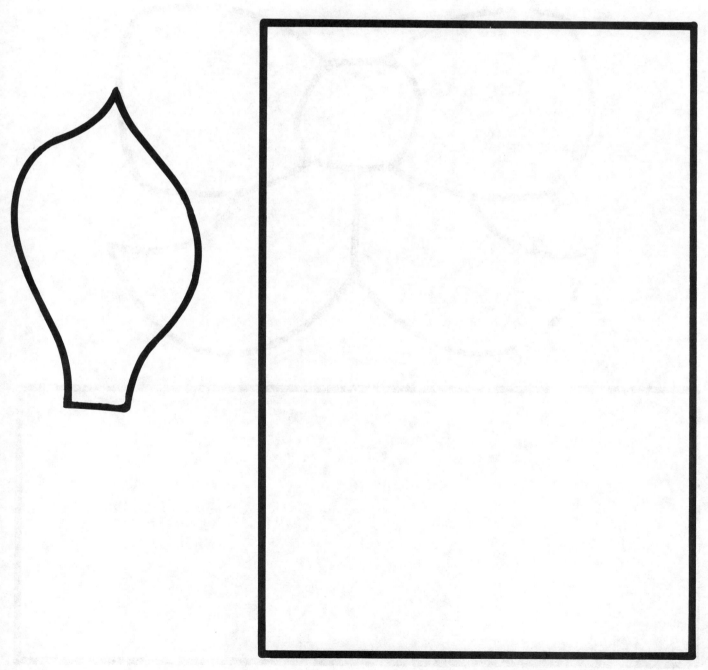

PRESENT

WINTER

Skills: Solid, straight lines, small curves
Steps: Cutting, pasting
Suggestions: Cover the box with gift wrap before adding the bow.
Literature Link: *The Christmas Box*
by Eve Merriam
There is only one present for the whole family under the Christmas tree.

REINDEER

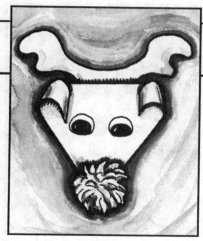

Skills: Straight lines, circle, curved lines
Steps: Cutting, coloring, pasting
Suggestions: Paste a red fringe ball to the nose.
Literature Link: *How the Reindeer Saved Santa*
  by Carolyn Haywood
Santa's thinking of trading the sleigh for
a helicopter.

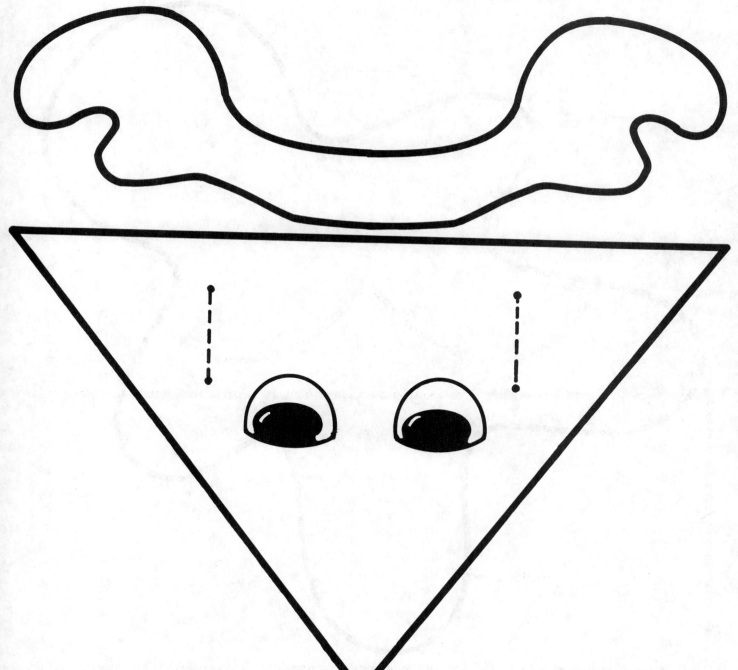

WINTER

GINGERBREAD

Skills: Curves
Steps: Coloring, finger painting, gluing, cutting
Suggestions: Finger paint colored icing. Add button, yarn detail.
Literature Link: *The Gingerbread Rabbit*
by Randall Jarrell
A gingerbread rabbit escapes baking but is almost eaten by a fox.

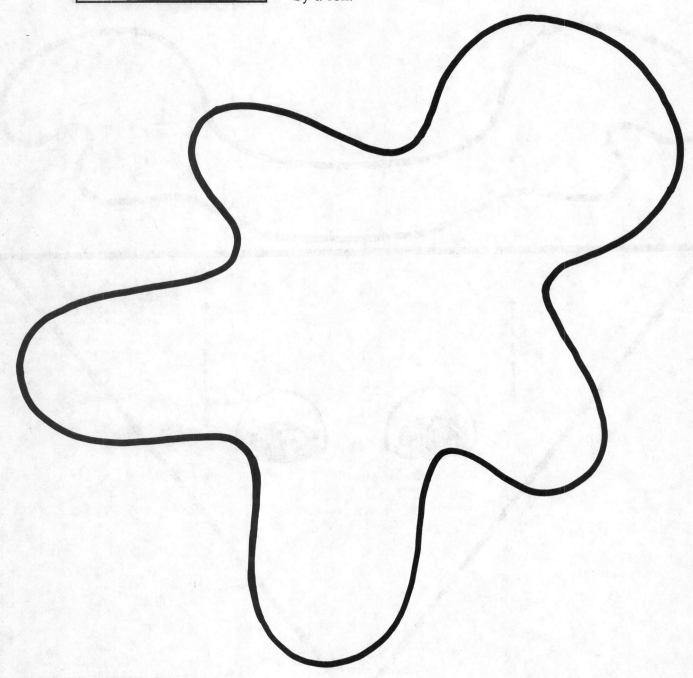

PENGUIN

WINTER

Skills: Large curves, angles
Steps: Cutting, tracing, pasting
Suggestions: Trace and cut patterns from construction paper. Assemble as shown. Fold beak in half before pasting.
Literature Link: *Funny Feet!*
by Leatie Weiss
Priscilla, the penguin, tries to cure her awkwardness.

WINTER

DRAGON

Skills: Large curves, zigzag lines
Steps: Cutting, coloring, folding, pasting
Suggestions: Color dragon and fold on dotted line. Paste tail in place.
Literature Link: *The Dragon of Og*
by Rumer Godden
   Ordinarily peaceful, a dragon has trouble getting along with the new lord.

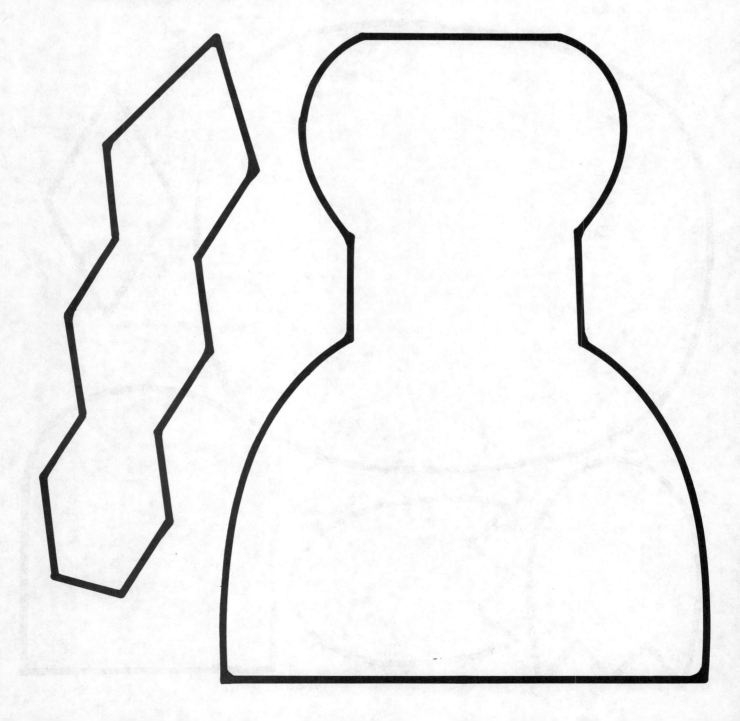

POLAR BEAR

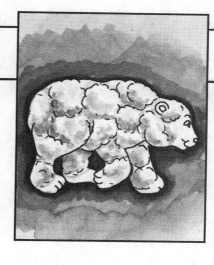

WINTER

Skills: Curves—large and small
Steps: Cutting, pasting
Suggestions: Glue cotton balls or cotton batting to resemble fur.
Literature Link: *White Bear, Ice Bear*
by Joanne Ryder
A boy is transformed into a polar bear in the snowy landscape.

WINTER

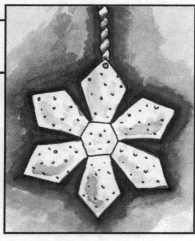

SNOWFLAKE

Skills: Small angles
Steps: Cutting, gluing, sprinkling
Suggestions: Spread glue on the snowflake. Sprinkle with sparkling glitter.
Literature Link: *Simon and the Snowflakes*
by Gilles Tibo
Young Simon likes to count snowflakes as they fall.

LOVEBIRDS

Skills: Solid straight, curved lines
Steps: Cutting, overlapping, gluing, decorating
Suggestions: Fold hearts in half. Overlap and glue. Decorate with trims.
Literature Link: *Bird Song Lullaby*
by Diane Stanley
A young girl gets her wish when she wonders what it would be like to be a bird.

BROKEN HEART

Skills: Large curves, zigzag lines
Steps:
Suggestions: Cut apart heart on zigzag line. Separate and paste to construction paper.
Literature Link: *Don't Be My Valentine*
by Joan M. Lexau
Sam gets his valentines mixed up and sends them to the wrong people.

PAW PRINT

Skills: Large and small curves
Steps: Cutting, gluing, paint printing
Suggestions: Glue paw to one half of folded construction paper. Make hand paint-prints on other half.
Literature Link: *The Valentine Bears*
by Eve Bunting
Mr. and Mrs. Bear decide not to sleep through Valentine's Day this year.

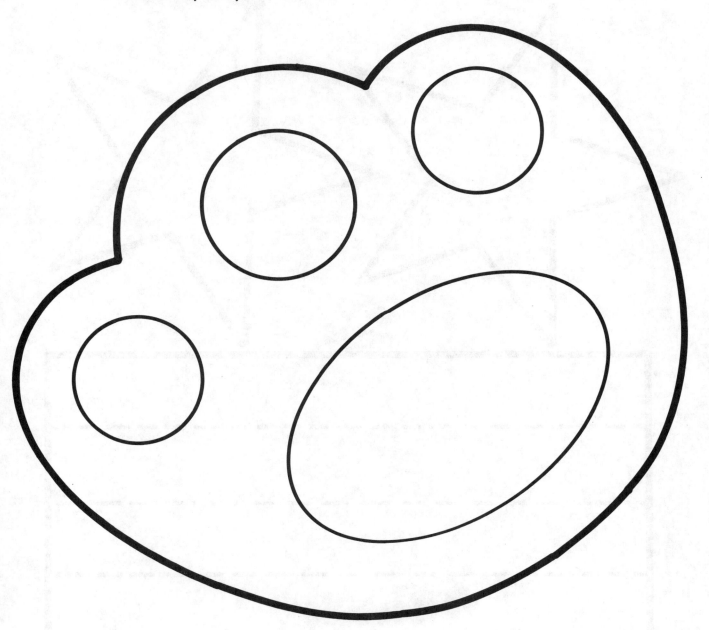

WINTER

STARS & STRIPES

Skills: Dotted straight lines, angles
Steps: Cutting, coloring, pasting
Suggestions: Color patriotic stars and stripes. Paste to contrasting paper.
Literature Link: *Draw Me a Star*
by Eric Carle
A variety of drawings start with a simple star.

CUPCAKE

Skills: Solid straight lines, scallops
Steps: Cutting, painting, gluing
Suggestions: "Frost" the cupcake with finger paint. Glue on a real birthday candle.
Literature Link: *A Birthday Cake for Little Bear* by Max Velthuijs
Everyone wants to sample Little Bear's cake.

WINTER

PEPPERMINT

Skills: Large curves, small angles
Steps: Cutting, finger painting
Suggestions: Finger paint red swirls in the peppermint.
Literature Link: *The Sweet Touch*
                    by Lorna Balian
   Genie's spell causes everything Peggy touches to turn to candy.

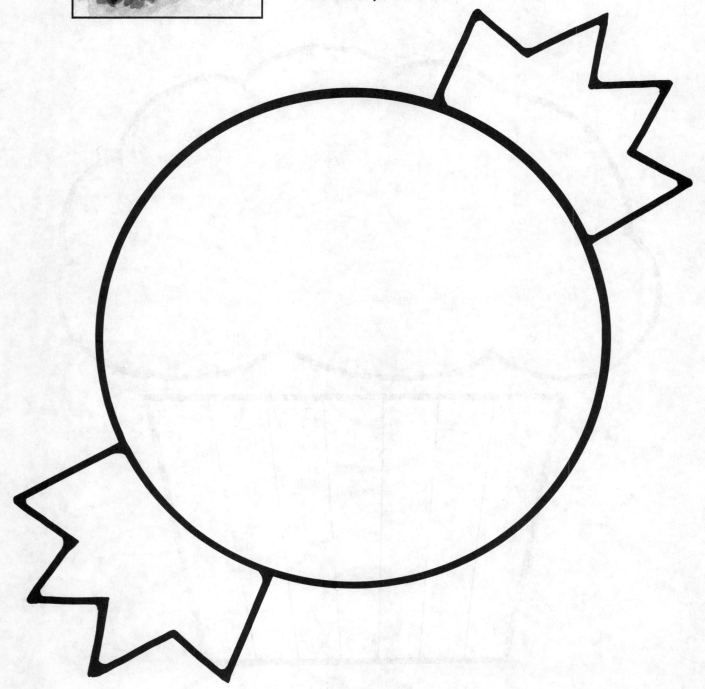

WOOLY LAMB

SPRING

Skills: Small circle, small spirals
Steps: Cutting, coloring, pasting
Suggestions: Color a landscape. Paste cut-outs to form lamb's body. Color feet.
Literature Link: *Lambing Time*
by Jane Miller
Follows the first two weeks in the lives of twin lambs.

SPRING

LEPRECHAUN

Skills: Straight solid lines, straight dotted lines, curved lines
Steps: Cutting, coloring, pasting
Suggestions: Roll into tube and paste to hold. Curl bottom
   fringed edge around a pencil.
Literature Link: *Elfabet*
         by J. Yolen
   Impish characters take a trip through the alphabet.

LION

SPRING

Skills: Large circles, short dotted lines
Steps: Cutting, pasting, coloring
Suggestions: Curl fringed edges. Paste yarn
  pieces to mane.
Literature Link: *Forget Me Knot*
          by Paul Rogers
A story about an absent-minded lion.

SPRING

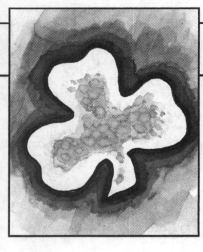

SHAMROCK

Skills: Curves
Steps: Cutting, finger painting
Suggestions: Finger paint a green shamrock before cutting it out.
Literature Link: *St. Patrick's Day in the Morning*
by Eve Bunting
A small boy has a St. Patrick's Day adventure.

CURLY PIG

SPRING

Skills: Large circle, small spiral
Steps: Cutting, painting, pasting
Suggestions: Finger paint a brown background or spread real mud. Paste the pig in the mud.
Literature Link: *The Pigs' Wedding* by Helme Heine
Curlytail and Porker say "I do".

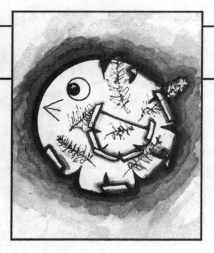

CHICK

Skills: Large circle, straight line, small curve, fringing
Steps: Cutting, watercolor painting, gluing
Suggestions: Watercolor downy feathers. Curl fringed edges. Glue wing to body.
Literature Link: *Little Chicken*
       by Margaret Wise Brown
   The story of a newly hatched chicken and her search for friends.

BUNNY

SPRING

Skills: Large scallops
Steps: Cutting, coloring, gluing
Suggestions: Glue a fluffy cotton-ball tail to the bunny.
Literature Link: *The Country Bunny and the Little Gold Shoes* by DuBose Heyward
The Mother of 21 bunnies realizes her ambition to be an Easter Bunny.

SPRING

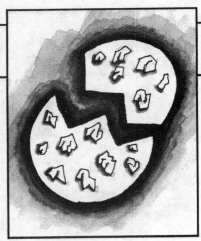

CRACKED EGG

Skills: Large oval, zigzag lines
Steps: Cutting, coloring, gluing
Suggestions: Spread glue over part of the egg. Sprinkle with crushed eggshell.
Literature Link: *Just Plain Fancy*
by Patricia Polacco
Amish sisters find an abandoned egg ready to hatch.

CARROT

SPRING

Skills: Small scallops
Steps: Cutting, painting, gluing
Suggestions: Paint "dirt" on one half of a piece of paper. Glue the carrot above and below ground level.
Literature Link: *Where Is It?*
　　　　　　　by Tana Hoban
Photographs show a rabbit searching for food.

SPRING

RAIN CLOUD

Skills: Large scallops, small curves
Steps: Cutting, painting, gluing
Suggestions: Watercolor a rain cloud. Hang drops from the cloud with blue yarn.
Literature Link: *Jonathan's Cloud* by Gardner McFall
　　A boy tries to find a way to keep the cloud that floated through his bedroom window.

BASKET

Skills: Large curves, small ovals
Steps: Cutting, coloring, pasting
Suggestions: Color pretty eggs to paste in the basket.
Literature Link: *The Easter Egg Artists*
by Adrienne Adams
A rabbit family paints 100 dozen eggs in preparation for Easter baskets.

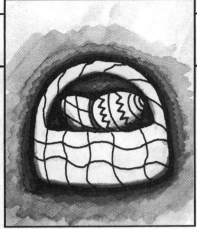

SPRING

SPIDER

Skills: Large oval, dotted straight lines
Steps: Cutting, counting, gluing, folding
Suggestions: Count eight legs. Glue four on each side. Fold leg ends toward body. Fold in half to stand.
Literature Link: *One Hungry Spider*
by Jeannie Baker
The activities of spiders are used in this counting book.

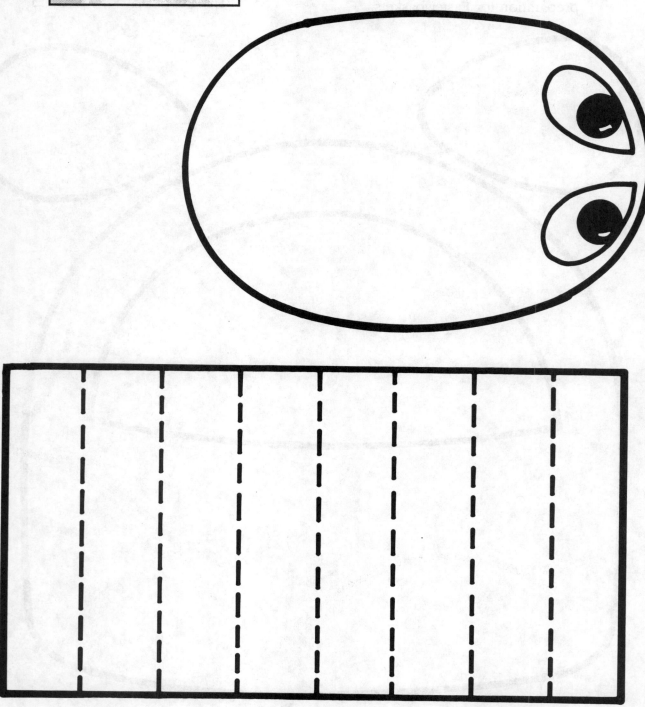

WEB

SPRING

Skills: Curved lines

Steps: Cutting, gluing

Suggestions: Cut 5-7 lengths of string. Dip in glue; squeeze out excess. Press into web shape.

Literature Link: *The Very Busy Spider*
by Eric Carle
A spider spins its web in this picture book.

SPRING

GREEN GRASS

Skills: Solid straight lines, fringing
Steps: Cutting, coloring, pasting
Suggestions: Color an outdoor scene. "Plant" grass. Cut colorful bugs to paste in the grass.
Literature Link: *The Grouchy Ladybug*
by Eric Carle
A grouchy ladybug travels among giant blades of grass.

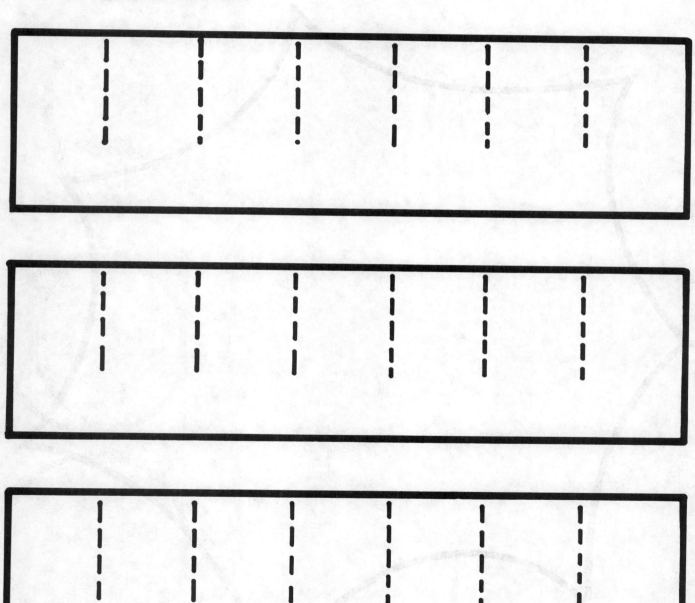

VASE

SPRING

Skills: Large curve, small circle, scallop, spiral
Steps: Cutting, coloring, pasting
Suggestions: Create a flower arrangement. Add pipe cleaner stems bent at different angles.
Literature Link: *Planting a Rainbow* by Lois Ehlert
A color-based introduction to the world of flowers.

SPRING

TULIP

Skills: Large curve, solid straight, small angles
Steps: Cutting, coloring, pasting
Suggestions: Create a cooperative tulip mural.
Literature Link: *The Boy Who Held Back the Sea*
by Lenny Hort
A story of a little boy who saves Holland; features landscapes.

SUN

Skills: Angles
Steps: Cutting, painting
Suggestions: Paint a yellow sun. While still wet, sprinkle with orange or gold glitter.
Literature Link: *The Miser Who Wanted the Sun*
             by Jurg Obrist
  A miser wants a golden robe so he will be like the sun.

SUMMER

SUMMER

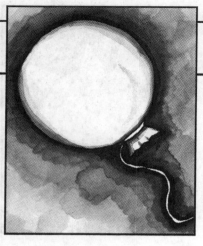

BALLOON

Skills: Large oval
Steps: Cutting, coloring, tying a knot
Suggestions: Tie a string to the end of the balloon.
Literature Link: *Louella and the Yellow Balloon*
by Joanne Ryder
    Mama pig tells Louella to hold on to the string of her balloon.

PIZZA

SUMMER

Skills: Large curved circle
Steps: Cutting, coloring, pasting
Suggestions: Cut and paste or color pizza ingredients on the crust.
Literature Link: *How Pizza Came to Queens* by Dayal Kaur Khalsa
   A young girl is introduced to pizza by an Italian visitor.

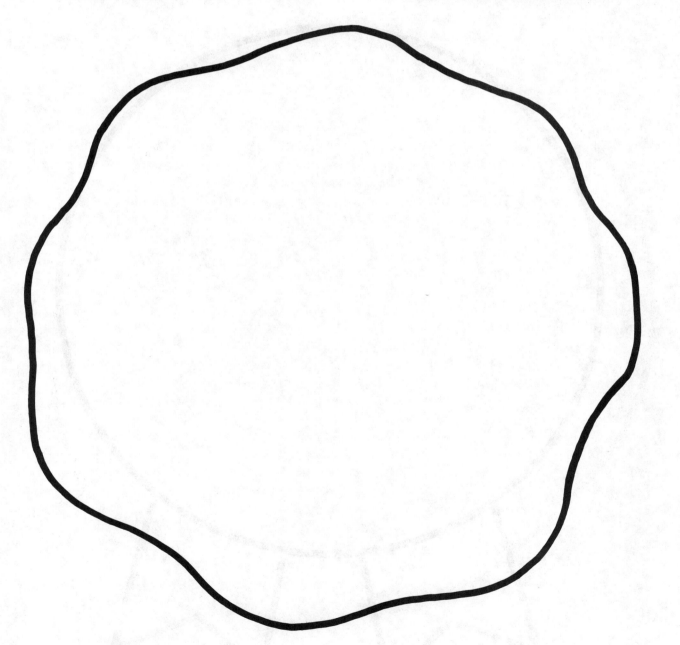

64

SUMMER

BLUE RIBBON

Skills: Large circle, angles
Steps: Cutting, coloring, pasting
Suggestions: Decorate the prize ribbon. Pin to student's collar or shirt.
Literature Link: *Brave Irene*
                    by William Steig
    Irene could win a ribbon for bravery for making a difficult journey through a snowstorm.

PRETZEL

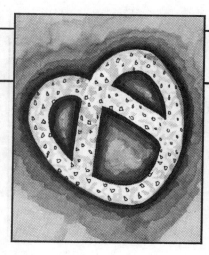

SUMMER

Skills: Large curve
Steps: Cutting, coloring, gluing, sprinkling
Suggestions: Use fingertips to spread glue on the colored pretzel. Sprinkle with kosher salt.
Literature Link: *Pretzel*
by Margaret Rey
A dachshund named Pretzel woos the dog across the street.

SUMMER

ROOT BEER

Skills: Solid straight lines, scallops
Steps: Cutting, coloring, painting, gluing
Suggestions: Sponge-paint a foamy top. Glue a real straw in the root beer float.
Literature Link: *The Great Cherry Migration* by Bruce Balan
    Soda fountain cherries attempt an escape—with interesting results!

TURTLE

Skills: Curves, straight dotted line
Steps: Cutting, overlapping, pasting
Suggestions: Sponge paint a green textured shell.
Literature Link: *Box Turtle at Long Pond*
by William George
Follow a turtle's day from beginning to end.

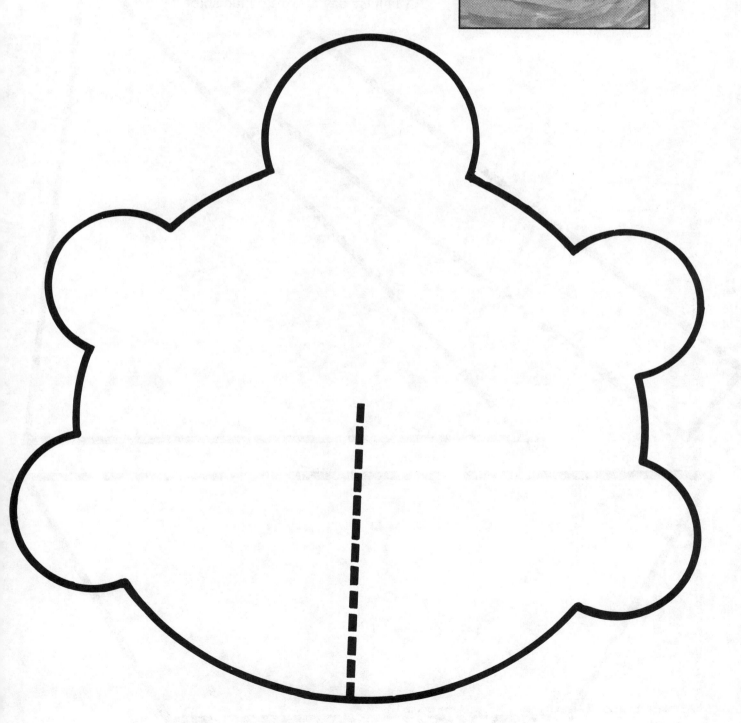

SUMMER

SAILBOAT

Skills: Solid straight lines, angles
Steps: Cutting, pasting
Suggestions: Paste a popsicle stick to the back of the mast
to make it sturdier.
Literature Link: *The Maggie B*
by Irene Haas
A fantasy day aboard a little ship.

LOLLIPOP

SUMMER

Skills: Large circle
Steps: Cutting, finger painting, gluing
Suggestions: Finger paint colorful swirls. Glue lollipop to a straw or popsicle stick.
Literature Link: *Lollipop*
    by Wendy Watson
    A small rabbit goes to the store to try and buy a lollipop.

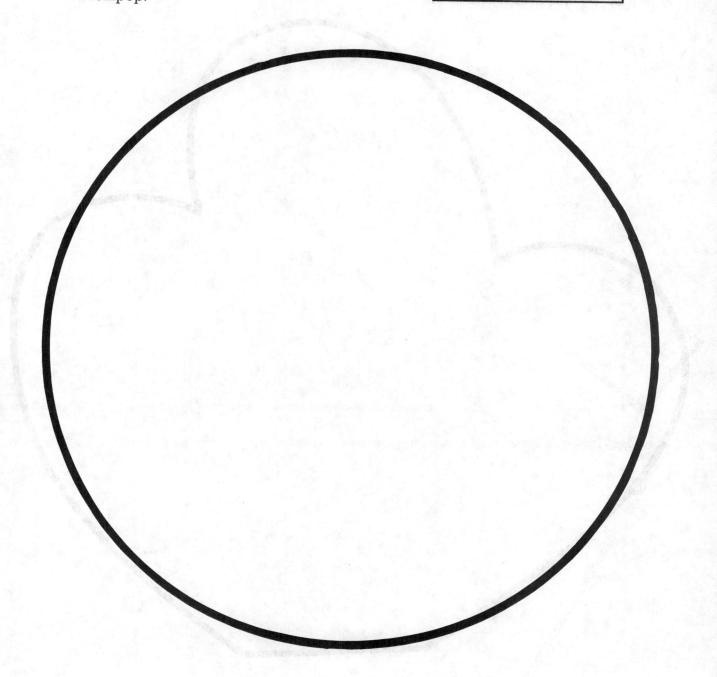

SUMMER

CACTUS

Skills: Curved lines
Steps: Cutting, coloring, pasting
Suggestions: Paste toothpicks to resemble spines.
Literature Link: *Clementina's Cactus*
by Ezra Jack Keats
A girl is curious about a cactus plant she sees.

GUMBALLS

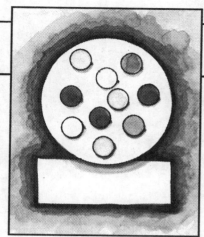

SUMMER

Skills: Large circle, small circle, straight lines
Steps: Cutting, pasting, identifying
Suggestions: Cut small circles in every color.
Paste in the gumball machine. Identify the colors.
Literature Link: *Of Colors and Things*
        by Tana Hoban
Colors explained in picture book style.

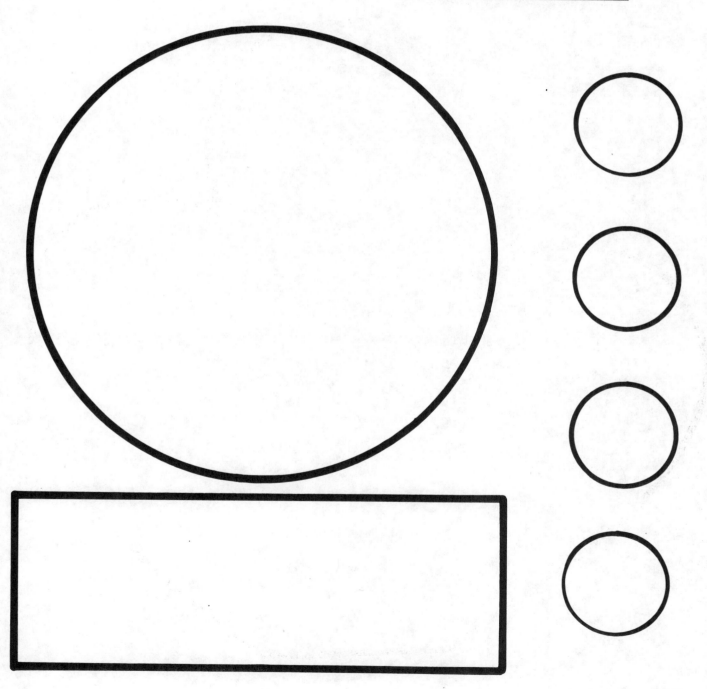